An entertaining and historically important collection, this work provides a unique perspective on one of the most important moments in Church history, and gives a much needed human touch to the Council. A must-read!

—✠ MOST REV ANTHONY FISHER OP, *Archbishop of Sydney*

On all sides, scholars have treated the Second Vatican Council with stern and somber gravity. These cleverly translated Latin limericks, with their references to tedious prattle, clerical ambition, long-winded speeches, and the refuge of the local tavern, are therefore a breath of fresh air. There is no doubt that something happened at the Council, and it is a delight to realize that one of the things that happened was laughter at human foibles and pomposity!

—DR MATTHEW LEVERING, *James N. and Mary D. Perry Jr. Chair of Theology, Mundelein Seminary*

A unique, historically fascinating, and utterly entertaining light on the life of Vatican II. A remarkable historical document, beautifully produced and eruditely edited.

—DR STEPHEN BULLIVANT, *Professor of Theology and the Sociology of Religion (Director, Benedict XVI Centre for Religion and Society), St Mary's University, Twickenham, UK*

A Limerickal Commentary on the Second Vatican Council

Limericks composed by the English Bishops
during the Second Vatican Council
Given to S.F.C. by
Archbp. Patrick Dwyer —

A
Limerickal
Commentary
ON THE
Second Vatican Council

Edited & Annotated by
HUGH SOMERVILLE
KNAPMAN OSB
Foreword by George Cardinal Pell

AROUCA
PRESS

In Association with
The Weldon Press, Woolhampton

ISBN: 978-1-989905-17-3 (pbk)
ISBN: 978-1-989905-18-0 (hardcover)

Arouca Press
PO Box 55003
Bridgeport PO
Waterloo, ON N2J3G0
Canada
www.aroucapress.com
Send inquiries to info@aroucapress.com

Book and cover design by
Michael Schrauzer

For
John Knapman
27/7/57–27/7/57

Fratri ignoto sed tamen carissimo

CONTENTS

PREFACE

WHILE RESEARCHING OTHER MATTERS in the archives of Stanbrook Abbey early in 2020 I came across a typescript among the papers of Dame Felicitas Corrigan (1908–2003), an English Benedictine nun of wide acquaintance and no little renown. The typescript's cover bears the (not wholly accurate, it turns out) note in Dame Felicitas' hand, "Limericks composed by the English Bishops during the Second Vatican Council Given to S.F.C. by Archbp. Patrick Dwyer". It seems that more than one copy was made as the present abbot of Douai was given a similar typescript by Dame Felicitas ("S.F.C.") when he was chaplain at Stanbrook in the 1990s.

The precise motivation behind this compilation remains a mystery for now, as does the background to Bishop Wall's Latin translations. The Covid pandemic has precluded visits to archives for the duration. However, Dame Felicitas' consoror, Dame Margaret Truran, reports that Archbishop Dwyer's acquaintance with Dame Felicitas dated from at least 1969 when Archbishop Dwyer, the local ordinary, visited Stanbrook and was charmed by the vernacular setting of the Mass being sung by the nuns on the Third Sunday after Epiphany. It was Dame Felicitas who had adapted the Latin chants of the *Graduale*, and on learning this the archbishop asked her to compose a vernacular setting for the televised celebration Mass on the following Third Sunday of Lent at St Chad's cathedral in Birmingham.

Thereafter Sr Felicitas would send Archbishop Dwyer copies of her circulars or books, and it is likely that he sent her the typescript of the conciliar limericks as a response in kind. He shared with Dame Felicitas a sadness at the demise of the Latin liturgy and a desire to prevent what appeared to be the imminent loss of many devotional prayers. When bidding prayers were introduced into the Mass it was Archbishop Dwyer who suggested that they conclude with the congregational recitation of the Hail Mary, so that the faithful might not forget this ancient prayer. The practice is now widespread in England.

As I make ready to research the liturgical first-fruits of the Council, it seemed a pity that these limericks (and concluding verse not in the limerick form) were not more widely known. They offer an insight into the experience of at least some of the anglophone bishops at the Council, as well as a testimony to their humanity and wit. In Bishop Bernard Wall's case, they witness to a knowledge of Latin of which we see far less in these enlightened days, even among the clergy. The limericks also offer a contemporaneous micro-commentary on some of the personalities and issues at the Council, adding a dash of colour to later and more conventional, wider-ranging and profounder commentary. The limericks reveal that bishops were exercised most, perhaps not surprisingly, by matters affecting themselves.

Any native of Australia—like myself—will be pleased to see that the most prolific limericist was the Bishop of Darwin. Ecclesiastical backwater though Darwin might seem, its bishop was not lacking in erudition and wit. Moreover, he could well stand as a typical anglophone bishop from the new world at the Council—able to engage with the issues, often surprised by some of the speakers, irritated by a few, and amused by others. Like many anglophone bishops, he seems to have been unprepared for, and not wholly sympathetic with, the king-tide that flowed from the Rhine into the Tiber from 1962.

Even those well versed in modern theology and Church history may find some references in the limericks a little obscure, so some effort has been expended to provide notes that give some context to the people, issues and events touched on in the limericks. Deciding what notes to supply has been a challenge in itself, and in supplying them brevity has been sought; the limericks are the focus, not the notes. One limerick's specific context (if there is one) still evades me. Those with a knowledge of Latin will enjoy Bishop Wall's deft translations, not least the onomatopoeic Latin of limerick XVII. He is one among many witnesses to the fact that Latin is no dead language.

A few of these limericks have surfaced here and there in various works on the Council, sometimes with attributions that differ from those supplied here, or with no attribution at all. Given the care with which the original typescript was compiled, originating from a leading English Council Father, it seems justifiable to accept the precise attributions for the various limericks supplied therein.

This text has been reproduced faithfully from the typescript; the few corrections are duly noted. Thanks must go to Mother Anna Brennan, Abbess of Stanbrook, and her community for agreeing to the publication of this charming, and occasionally poignant, supplement to the history of the Second Vatican Council. Dame Margaret Truran's enlightening reminiscences also merit gratitude. Likewise, the editor is grateful to His Eminence, George Cardinal Pell, for taking an interest in this little volume. My thanks also to Dr Brian Sudlow of Aston University, Dr Stephen Morgan of the University of St Joseph in Macau, and Mr Andrew Leigh of Winchester College for their assistance with my own translations, and to Mr Alexandros Barbas of Arouca Press for enabling the limerickal commentary on the Council to be enjoyed by a wider audience. Lastly, my thanks and blessings go to all who have encouraged this project.

Fruaris lector!

Hugh Somerville Knapman OSB
St Elizabeth's, Scarisbrick

FOREWORD

THESE LIMERICKS AND THEIR LATIN translations take us back to a world that has vanished: where Trent was dominant, the Beatles and the contraceptive pill had just arrived and many bishops, priests and seminarians had a command of Church Latin. Some could also write humorously; no mean achievement.

As a seminarian in Rome for three of the Council sessions, I remember these verses emerging, admired by the student body, but met with a whiff of disapproval by the most zealous reformers. It is good they are reappearing.

✠ George Cardinal Pell
Collegio de Propaganda Fide (1963–7)
Rome

FACETIAE . QVAEDAM

LIMERICENSES . QVAS . VOCANT

DE . QVIBVSDAM . IN . CONCILIO . VATICANO . II

DICTIS . VEL . GESTIS

COMMENTARIOLA

HAVDQVAQVAM . SANE . ACTIS . INSERENDA

A . VARIIS . AVCTORIBVS . ANGLICE . CONFECTAE

IN . LINGVAM . VERSAE . LATINAM

A . RSSMO . DNO . BERNARDO . PATRICIO . WALL

EPISCOPO . BRENTVOODENSI

AB . AN . MCMLXII . AD . MCMLXV

A. A Rssmo Ioanne Patricio O'Loughlin, Epo. Darvinen, Australia

I

Of Rahner and Congar and Kung
the praises are everywhere sung;
　　but one bello domani
　　Lord Ottaviani
will see all three of 'em hung.

Rahneri, vae! Kunghi, Congari
audimus iam laudes cantari;
　　at iubebis cras mane,
　　mi Octaviane,
mox laqueum istis mandari.

II

Said Suenens in one congregation,
'I'm firmly against segregation.
　　The Bishops aren't churls,
　　let's bring in the girls;
so what, if it cause consternation?'

Ait Suenens Vaticano in coetu,
'Hoc schismate irrigor fletu.
　　Haud rudes nos Patres,
　　consedeant Matres,
nec carpentium simus in metu'.

III

Our Secretary's not sympathetic
to an expert that's peripatetic.
　　He thinks a peritus
　　should stick to his situs,
except when he's really dyspeptic.

Ex animo Felix phrenetico
perito ait peripatetico,
　　'A propria sede
　　ne vagus discede,
ni haustu turberis emetico'.

IV

The Coadjutors are very intent
lest their Bishops whose lives are
　　　　　　　　far spent
　　in a moment neurotic
　　take an antibiotic
without their advice and consent.

Nunc praecavent Coadiutores
ne Antistites iam seniores
　　prae crisi neurotica
　　sumant antibiotica
inconsulte, et sint sibi maerores.

SOME AMUSING

"LIMERICKS"

Concerning certain Things
said and done
AT THE

Second
VATICAN COUNCIL

A COMMENTARY
that must absolutely *not* be
included in the *Official Record.*

By various AUTHORS.

The *English* being
rendered into *Latin,*

By the Most Reverend

BERNARD PATRICK WALL,

Lord Bishop of BRENTWOOD,[1]
between 1962 *and* 1965[2]

FACETIÆ QVÆDAM

LIMERICENSES

Qvas Vocant
de QVIBVSDAM *in*

CONCILIO VATICANO II

Dictis vel Gestis
COMMENTARIOLA
havdqvaqvam sane *Actis Inserenda.*

A Variis AVCTORIBVS.

Anglice confectæ in
Lingvam Versæ *Latinam,*

A Rssmo Dno
BERNARDO PATRICIO WALL

Episcopo BRENTVOODENSI
ab AN MCMLXII *ad* MCMLXV

{A}

By *the Most Rev'd*
JOHN PATRICK O'LOUGHLIN,[3]
Bishop of Darwin, Australia

I

Of Rahner and Congar and Küng[4]
the praises are everywhere sung;
  but one bello domani
  Lord Ottaviani
will see all three of 'em hung.

II

Said Suenens[5] in one congregation,
"I'm firmly against segregation.
  The Bishops aren't churls,
  Let's bring in the girls;
so what, if it cause consternation?"

III

Our Secretary's[6] not sympathetic
to an expert that's peripatetic.
  He thinks a *peritus*
  should stick to his *situs,*
except when he's really dyspeptic.

{A}

A *Rssmo*
IOANNE PATRICIO O'LOUGHLIN,
Epo. Darvinen, Australia

I

Rahneri, væ! Kunghi, Congari
audimus iam laudes cantari;
at iubebis cras mane,
mi Octaviane,
mox laqueum istis mandari.

II

Ait Suenens Vaticano in cœtu,
"Hoc schismate irrigor fletu.
Haud rudes nos Patres,
consedeant Matres,
nec carpentium simus in metu."

III

Ex animo Felix phrenetico
perito ait peripatetico,
"A propria sede
ne vagus discede,
ni haustu turberis emetico."

IV

The Coadjutors[7] are very intent
lest their Bishops whose lives are far spent
    in a moment neurotic
    take an antibiotic
without their advice and consent.

V

We are two thousand Fathers in session,
who feel a great weight of oppression,
    what with Cardinals talking
    and lesser lights squawking,
thank goodness the bar's so refreshin'.

VI

We all admit that the deacon[8]
could shine in the Church like a beacon;
    But...with a celibate's vows,
    or a man with a spouse?
that's the question whose answer we're seekin'.

VII

There was a young bishop from Spain
who would not from speaking refrain.
    But he went much too fast,
    from the first to the last
the rest found his Latin a strain.

IV

Nunc præcavent Coadiutores
ne Antistites iam seniores
  præ crisi neurotica
  sumant antibiotica
inconsulte, et sint sibi mærores.

V

Bis mille nos Patres sedemus,
atque auribus vim sustinemus,
  purpuratis garrientibus
  et vulgaribus stridentibus,
in taberna nos iam recreemus.

VI

Diaconi in Ecclesia Cari
elucerent sane uti phari,
  at an cælibes rati,
  an uxore ornati?
En quæstio, en questus amari.

VII

Antistes hispanicus tam celere
verba cocta in fauces impellere,
  ut ab ovis ad poma,
  etsi gustantes aroma,
haud latinum possemus digerere.

VIII

Some think the Episcopal Conference[9]
Wouldn't show the Ordinary due deference;
    for though the Church is hierarchical,
    it's also monarchical,
and to this the Council should make reference.

IX

Call us comrades or cobbers or mates,
or even buddies, the term in the States;
    secure in the knowledge
    we belong to the College,
with the Pope we're to have tête-à-têtes.

X

Cardinal Bacci,[10] our great expert in Latin
took his stand one fine day at the battin',
    on the sticky wicket
    of ecumenical cricket,
but his stumps the Moderator did flatten.

XI

What John Carmel, Westminster's Archbish,[11]
dislikes most intensely is fish
    he's not slow in declaring
    he can't stand red Häring,[12]
it just simply isn't his dish.

VIII

Cœtusne episcopalis institutio
Ordinario fit capitis deminutio?
    etsi Ecclesia hierarchica,
    est etiam monarchica;
a Concilio iam detur attributio.

IX

Vel socios nos appelles vel sodales,
vel comites vel contubernales,
    collegiati cum simus,
    penes Papam inimus
colloquium velut inter æquales.

X

Noster Bacchus se sivit intrudi
œcumenici luteo ludi;
    quem cum sphæra coniecta
    sit obex disiecta,
iussit arbiter Præses extrudi.

XI

Vestmónasteriensis Henanus,
vir omni viventi humanus,
    pisces respuit nimis,
    et (H)aringum imprimis;
minus displicet stomachus vanus.

XII

A young titular bishop auxiliary[13]
serves the Church in a fashion subsidiary;
    he was kept in the cooler
    by his Episcopal Ruler
in a kind of clerical penitentiary.

XIII

There are some who affirm collegiality
will give the Church much greater vitality;
    but Ruffini[14] of Palermo
    in a powerful *sermo*
denied it had any reality.

XIV

To force an ancient bishop to resign
is considered by the Council not benign:
    only secular planners
    with no christian manners
would a churchman to oblivion assign.[15]

XV

Bishop Hervas[16] has made the proposal
that Coadjutors are ripe for disposal;
    for it's hardly humane
    that a man should remain
without definite hopes of espousal.[17]

XII

Servit episcopus auxiliarius
Ecclesiæ subsidiarius,
servandus Ordinario
velut in frigidario
vel in ergastulo uti nefarius.

XIII

Quod Episcopos collegium conflaret
Ecclesiam, sic aiunt, renovaret;
id non placuit Ruffino,
quia ex verbo divino
esse collegium haudquaquam constaret.

XIV

Pontificatu se senem abdicare
inhumanum id esset mandare:
mens hæc est Concilii;
sit mundani consilii
oblivioni episcopum dare.

XV

Sponsalibus iam Coadiutores,
ait Hervas, sunt maturiores
(cælestibus id est);
nam molestius quid est
quam sponsæ semper crepere fores?

XVI

Cardinal Cushing[18] of Boston avows
that he freedom to all men allows:
  though he's no Latin scholar,
  he can certainly holler:
at the Council he brought down the House.

XVII

From Texas came young Bishop Leven,[19]
where the shooters are six and not seven,
  saying, "They give me the pip!"
  he blazed away from the hip,
sending numerous Bishops to heaven.

XVIII

Ottaviani, Parente and Browne,[20]
ecclesiastics of no mean renown,
  are not slow to hit back
  at a Curia attack;
harsh criticism merits their frown.

XIX

The fault of the Doctrinal Commission[21]
is by no means a sin of omission:
  for Progressives are saddened
  and Conservatives gladdened
that everything needs its permission.

XVI

Clamitat Cushingus, "Libertas!
Sit omnium propria Libertas!"
  Etsi latine non fari,
  potest vociferari,
plausu ruit Aula: "Libertas!"

XVII

Prosiluit Levenus perlætum
vibrans sclop-pop-pop-pop-pop-pop-etum;
  in Episcopos arsit,
  eos glandibus sparsit;
qui cæleste nunc cernunt secretum.

XVIII

Octavianus, Bruno, Parente,
fama prælati ingente,
  non tardant repugnare
  audenti castigare
Curiam sermone nocente.

XIX

Doctrinalis peccatum Commissionis
haudquaquam est omissionis:
  en moderni mærentes,
  servatores gaudentes
quod vis poscitur permissionis.

XX

Dom Butler of Oxford just froze,
when Muldoon[22] of Sydney arose
    to rebuke the obsession
    some have with confession:
"In the Colonies everything goes."

XXI

In the Council there's mild perturbation,
since the Pope, after due consultation,
    to conciliar speeches
    now admits *auditrices*,
but the ladies feel great jubilation.[23]

XXII

It's reported that three Latin nations
have monopolised canonizations;
    it seems rather quaint
    that a non-Latin saint
gets a halo with some limitations.

XXIII

Some moralists claim that the Pill
may be used even though you're not ill.
    It gives the ability
    to banish fertility;
but I can't really think it's God's will.

XX

Cum Muldunus Sydneyensis exstaret
et Pænitentia anxos increparet,
   Oxoniensis Butlerus
   ait frigens, severus,
"In Coloniis fieri quidvis apparet."

XXI

In Concilio sat Patres turbantur
cum Pontificis nutu admittantur
   monachæ et matres
   ad audiendos Patres:
de quo ipsæ vehementer lætantur.

XXII

Putant gentes latinæ deberi
cælestes honores censeri
   suis civibus tantum:
   at ceteris quantum?
num coronas stramineas præberi?

XXIII

Sunt moralistæ qui audeant docere
et a sana sumi licere
   pastillam qua reddatur
   sterilis; at quæratur
num valeat id Deo placere.

XXIV

There was solemn and long disputation
on the founts of divine Revelation;
    there used to be two,
    but when under review,
they have suffered a grave mutilation.[24]

XXV

Some theologians with keen exposition
seem intent on destroying Tradition:
    on Theology's new wave
    they ride very brave,
but they really lack true erudition.

XXVI

The Greeks have the head of Saint Andrew,[25]
its return is long overdue.
    But I am sorry to state
    that Ruffini's pate
Progressives are now claiming too.

XXVII

Maximos in the Patriarch's bench,[26]
whose ardour no mortal can quench,
    gets quite temperamental
    about things oriental,
and makes fiery speeches in French.
[At this point a bell signals the end]

XXIV

Diuturna de Revelatione
peracta iam disceptatione,
   eius fontes olim binæ,
   recognitæ, in fine
Obscurantur, heu! confusione.

XXV

Doctrinæ quidam traditam veræ
memoriam voluntne delere?
   Quos gaudio affectos,
   novi æstibus vectos,
scientia tamen liquet egere.

XXVI

Nobis capite iamdiu credito
Andreæ, et Græcis mox reddito,
   proh dolorem Averni
   conclamitant Moderni:
"Nobis verticem Ruffini nunc dedito."

XXVII

Maximos e sede patriarchali
disputans de re orientali
   semper utitur verbis
   fervidissimis, acerbis,
et gallice, gallice, galli...
[Finem hic sonat tintinnabulum]

XXVIII

Schema thirteen[27] is vast in its scope,
it bravely endeavours to cope
    with all the world's ills,
    plus anovulant pills:
to complete it we haven't a hope.

XXIX

The Limerick's inferior, they say,
to the poetry of Shelley or Gray;
    but the Bishop of 'X'[28]
    without wishing to vex,
composes at least one a day.

XXX

Cardinal Alfrink,[29] who speaks for the Dutch,
thinks the Romans are quite out of touch.
    "If some writers are rash,
    the Church here won't crash;
I admit, though, we talk a bit much."

XXXI

In debating he shows he's tenacious,
his argument's seldom fallacious.
    One thing about Carli,[30]
    He's ready to parley:
indeed, some may think him loquacious.

XXVIII

De Huius Temporis Ecclesia decretum
omnia tractat apud Cœtum:
    res magnas et pusillas,
    anovulantes pastillas;
quod videndi spes nulla expletum.

XXIX

Etsi facetias Limericenses
poemata haud optima censes,
    saltem unam cotidie
    facit quidam, nec invidiæ,
et plausu gratulantur Darvinenses.

XXX

Alfrincus, qui Batavos defendit,
Romanos deesse prætendit:
    "Temeraria si quis scribit,
    num hæc Ecclesia peribit;
Verba nimis gens nostra dispendit."

XXXI

De Carlo, propositi tenaci,
nec sæpæ argumentis fallaci,
    eum saltem dicendum
    paratum ad colloquendum,
etsi ore aliquando loquaci.

XXXII

The white-headed Cardinal Cardijn[31]
Took the mike and said, "This is fine."
    But in his speech about JOC
    he neglected the clock,
and from pulpit was asked to resign.

XXXIII

Cardinal Suenens[32] considers that vows
made in church long ago by each spouse,
    if renewed once a year,
    would make partners more dear,
and reduce matrimonial rows.

XXXIV

I confess that I felt rather groggy
when the Eastern-rite Archbishop Zoghbi[33]
    though Christ's law is in force,
    made a plea for divorce,
if life's path for a spouse becomes boggy.

XXXV

Bishop Simons,[34] who comes from Indore,
has in Council seen fit to deplore
    that the plain teleology
    of human biology
makes binding the Natural Law.

XXXII

Cardinus stetit canus, purpuratus,
et microphonio sumpto, excitatus,
cum de IOCo dictitaret,
nec horologium servaret,
est pulpito descendere mandatus.

XXXIII

Coniuges, ait Suenens, si vota
iam pridem in ecclesia mota
quotannis novarent,
tunc amorem firmarent,
domique pax fieret tota.

XXXIV

Me fateor vehementer tædere
quod Zoghbius ausit urgere
contra Christi mandatum
fieri divortium ratum
quibus connubii naufragium fecere.

XXXV

Ausit Simon [sic] Indorensis adstare
in Concilio palamque plorare
quod e finibus certis
in hominem insertis
constat legam naturæ ligare.

XXXVI

In Council his task is to steer,
thank goodness his diction is clear;
    for Felici, ut patet,[34]
    our voting is Placet;
his Latin's a pleasure to hear.

XXXVII

Messrs Kaiser and Novak and Rynne[36]
have a grin that is now wearing thin:
    when asked for the cause,
    they say, "The applause
tells us Ottaviani will win."

XXXVIII

In St. Peter's there stood a Swiss Guard,
whose day at the Council was marred:
    he said, "I feel sore,
    this debate's about war,
and it's hard when my speech is debarred."

XXXIX

The Penitentiary Cardinal Cento[37]
re Indulgences said, "Please *memento*,
    there's some indignation
    at all the inflation
that's occurred in this matter since Trento."

XXXVI

Cum Felicis sit Cœtum gubernare,
Deo gratias quod loquitur clare.
    Sane illi ut patet
    suffragamur iam Placet:
Latinitatem hanc iuvat auscultare.

XXXVII

Nunc Cæsar, Novacus Rynnusque
non amplius arrident ut hucusque,
    quia palmam iam canus
    ferat Octavianus,
quod laudes demonstrant plaususque.

XXXVIII

Helvetiorum miles cohortis
stat genis mærore contortis,
    quod cum de bello tractatur,
    non ipse sinatur
quidquam tradere propriæ sortis.

XXXIX

Dixit Pænitentiarius Cento
de indulgentiarum momento,
    irritari haud raro
    vel plures de thesauro
a Tridentino inde distento.

XL: ENVOI

As we Bishops depart from old Roma,
we can proudly display our diploma.
    At the Council's finale
    we say, "Buon Natale"
and goodbye to Bar-Jonah's[38] aroma.

XL: VALETE!

Discendunt Episcopi Roma,
ostentantes suum quisque diploma;
nato Christo lætantes,
diffugiunt clamantes,
"Vale! Bar-Ionæ aroma."

{ B }

By the Most Rev'd
BERNARD PATRICK WALL,
Bishop of Brentwood

I
ON JOE'S BAR
IN THE VATICAN

To the Most Excellent and Most Reverend Lord
JOSEPH MCSHEA,[39] Bishop of *Allentown*,
having bestowed a great favour on us his colleagues
inasmuch as, we ourselves being worn
down by work in the Council and afflicted
with boredom by those prattling on,
he prepared and arranged this bar
signed with his name as a refuge and shelter;
for the sake of remembrance and in
consequence of a grateful heart,
we all, his coimbibers, sing praise.

12 *October* 1964
Session 3 of *Vatican* Council 2

A Bishop there was of the Town
called Allen,[40] and a man of renown,
    but far greater fame
    was his from the name
he gave to Joe's Bar. Now don't frown.

For though the bottles in colours all gay
stand like soldiers in battle array,
    the liquor we drink,
    or most of us, I think,
is black or a yellowish grey.

{B}

A *Rssmo Dno*
BERNARDO PATRICIO WALL,
Epo. Brentvooden

I
DE LOSEPHI TABERNA
IN VATICANO

EXCMO AC RSSMO DNO IOSEPHO MCSHEA
EPISCOPO ALANOPOLITANO
DE NOBIS EUIS COLLEGIS OPTIME MERITO
QVIPPE QVOD IPSIS
LABORE IN CONCILIO FRACTIS
GARRIENTIVMQVE TÆDIO AFFECTIS TABERNAM
HANC EIVS NOMINE INSIGNITAM
PERFVGIVM ET RECEPTACVLVM
COMPARAVIT DISPOSVITQVE
MEMORIAE CAVSSA ET GRATI ANIMI ERGO
LAVDES CONCINIMVS
COMBIBONES NOS VNIVERSI

D XII M OCTOBRI AN MDCCCCLXIV
CONCILI VATICANI II SESSIONE III

Antistes Alanopolitanus
clarescit iam capite canus;
  at clarior exstitit
  quod nomen præstitit
Ioseph Tabernæ. Nec ita profanus!

Nam ut lagenæ stent multicolores
velut acies, comminantes potores,
  nos nectar gustamus
  plerique (quod sciamus)
vel nigrum vel luteum. O mores!

II: THE PASSING OF A GREAT CHAMPION

With the gift of a great relic to Greece,
some whose names we will not release
   have now asked for the head
   of Ruffini, it's said,
for the sake of theological peace.

But Ruffini from rancour refrains,
and replies, "Yes, charity constrains:
   Ah well, this is it!
   but I gladly submit,
for it's the first time they'll have any brains."

III: THE LOWLY ORIGINS OF
THE ENGLISH BISHOPS

The following was suggested by an article that appeared in the *London Guardian* on the eve of the 4th Session of the Council (13-ix-65). It contained such remarks as "No Old Etonians or Harrovians figure in the Hierarchy...(which) is of uncompromisingly middle-class origins, and not by any means always from the upper middle class. For example, the late Cardinal Hinsley was the son of a village carpenter (!)...Catholic priests were once described by an Anglican as 'a rather rough and tricky lot, notoriously deficient in taste and manners.' If this is true of the rank and file, it could well apply to the Bishops."

THRENODY

Amid Fleet Street's bottles and jugs
we Bishops are less than the bugs
   that crawl up the seat on
   the scholar at Eton
we're just lower middle-class thugs.

II: PRÆCLARI ATHLETÆ TRANSITUS

Insignis Græcis capitis donati
exemplo, ut fertur, inflati,
    quidam caput exposcunt
    Ruffini, quem noscunt
doctrinæ obstare novitati.

Sed Ruffinus, nec torvis pupillis,
ait, "His subveniendum pusillis.
    Eia! de me est actum,
    at me submitto non fractum,
nam demum erit cerebrum illis."

III: DE EPISCOPORUM ANGLORUM
ORTU HUMILI

Eam quæ sequitur facetiam subiecit caput quiddam in
ephemeride The London Guardian pridie aperiendæ IV
Sessionis Concilii edito (d. xiii m. septembri,
mcccclxv). In quo talia emittuntur: "Inter Episcopos ne
ullus quidem ex studiorum domiciliis aut Etoniensi
aut Harroviensi effloruit . . . Omnes ex stirpe Prorsus
plebeia, imo quidam ex infima multitudine sunt orti.
Exempli caussa, felicis memoriæ Em. Cardinalis Hinsley
filius fuit fabri lignari et quidem rustici (!) . . . Descripsit
olim quidam Anglicanus sacerdotes Catholicos uti 'sat
rudes ac subdolos, et, quod Omnes norunt, insulsos,
inurbanos.' Quod si de ordine inferiori verum sit, nonne
forsan de ipsis Episcopis dici valeat?"

THRENUS

Ubi potant ephemeridum scriptores,
nos Episcopi æstimamur minores
    cimicibus obrepentibus
    Etoniensi et mordentibus:
plebeii et infimi grassatores.

{C}

By the Most Rev'd
GORDON WHEELER,[41]
Bishop of Theudalis

I: ON THE LOWLY ORIGINS OF THE ENGLISH BISHOPS, A REPLY

Hierarchical stratification
is a hazard of human creation;
    But we middle-class thugs
    (e'en though less than the bugs)
are the heart of the new dispensation.

II: ON THE BOOK ENTITLED 'OBJECTIONS TO ROMAN CATHOLICISM'[42]

I.

When the laity turn on the heat,
Bishops feel it is time to retreat;
    for it's futile to yell,
    "You go to Hell,"
when they think that the place is effete.

2.

Poor Ramsey[43] groaned under the rod
of Woolwich and 'Honest to God';
    but Heenan's own penchant
    for being quite trenchant
should deal with both Goffin and Todd.

{C}

A *Rssmo*

GORDONIO WHEELER,

Episcopo Theudalen

I: DE HUMILI ORTU EPISCOPORUM
ANGLORUM RESPONSIO

Hierarchica sæpe ordinatio
in humanis fit aleæ ratio;
    at nos plebeios grassatores,
    etsi cimicibus minores,
novi fœderis cor signat dispensatio.

II: DE LIBRO CUI INDEX 'QUÆ
DE RELIGIONIS CATHOLICA
IMPROBANDA'

1.

Cum laicus ore fervescit
recedens Antistes vanescit;
    nam quid prodest iubere
    se in tartaris torrere?
'Hæc fabula, ait, iam exolescit.'

2.

Ingemuit Ramseius prostratus
Vulvichii libro gravatus;
    at Henanus argutius
    frustrabit et tutius
Goffinæ Toddique conatus.

III: REPLY OF A PRINCE-ARCHBISHOP
TO THE ANTI-TRIUMPHALISM
OF PÈRE GAUTIER[44]

It's no use Père Gautier hootin',
for we'll always remain high-falutin':
    our crosses and rings
    are the vesture of kings;
so to hell with this wretched Rasputin!

IV: ON ADOPTING THE PHRASE
'YOU WHO' IN THE LITURGY,
ADVICE TO A HIERARCHY
BY G.P.D.[45]

If you're not going to put back the clock,
You should think of the ram with his flock:
    for we need every EWE,
    helped on by you know WHO,
to improve our liturgical stock.

III: IN GAUTIERUM
TRIUMPHALIUM EVERSOREM
SÆVAM INDIGNATIONEM
EXPRIMIT QUIDAM
ARCHIEPISCOPUS-PRINCEPS

Quam Gautieri sunt vani ululatus!
erit Antistes vir semper delicatus;
nam anuli, pectoralia
sunt ornamenta regalia;
Tollatur hic Rasputin sceleratus!

IV: DE VOCE 'YOU WHO' IN
RE LITURGICA USURPANDA
QUONDAM HIERARCHIAM
ADMONUIT G.P.D.

Ne forte huic tempori desitis,
purum stilum propagari velitis:
sonat vox, O VOS, oves,
at ubi aries, vos boves?
QVI sane, QVI bene scitis!

{D}

By the Most Rev'd
CYRIL COWDEROY,[46]
Archbishop of Southwark

HAIL TRIUMPHALISM

After drinks with the Irish one night,
the Prince Bishop felt very tight;
    but with the help of old Galway
    he'll keep from the poor way,
and always incline to the Right.

{D}

A *Rssmo*
CYRILLO COWDEROY,
Archiepiscopo Suthvarcen

SALVETE, TRIUMPHALIA!

Ea nocte cum Hibernicis sat potum,
Archiepiscopum Principem commotum
Galviensis sustentabat,
a fossa deflectabat
ad dextram inter nobiles totum.

{E}

By an
ANONYMOUS AUTHOR

There was an old priest of Dunleary
who stood on his head for the Kyrie;
    when someone asked why,
    he made the reply,
"It's the latest liturgical theory."

{E}

Ab
AUCTORE ANONYMO

Stetit presbyter senex Dunliriæ
sursum deorsom ad Kyrie;
  qui quærenti, "Quo ludis?"
  ait, "Vides, tu rudis,
novissimum liturgica in serie."

{F}

By *the* Most *Rev'd*
GEORGE PATRICK DWYER,
Archbishop of Birmingham

ON ADOPTING THE PHRASE
'YOU WHO'[47] IN THE LITURGY,
REPLY BY G.P.D.

Said St. Peter one day to St. Paul,
"I can't stand this new stuff at all:
what with Wheeler's 'Thou who'
and Dwyer's 'You too',
it's enough to drive God up the Wall."*

---

* The Irish family name *Wall* is derived from the Norman-Irish *De Vál*, Gaelic *De Bhál*, and therefore in Latin, *Vallis*, not *Murus*.

{F}

A *Rssmo*
GEORGIO PATRICIO DWYER,
Archiepiscopo Birminehamien

DE VOCE 'YOU WHO' IN
RE LITURGICA USURPANDA,
RESPONDIT G.P.D.

Ait Petrus Paulo, "Auscultare
novum strepitum non possum tolerare:
pipit 'Tu qui' Velerius,
latrat 'Vos, Vos' Duiverius:
Deus ipse se in Valle vult celare."[*]

---

[*] Hoc familiæ Hibernicæ cognomen de lingua Normanno-hibernica *De Vál*, gadelice *De Bhál*, cum sit flexum, in latinum vertitur *Vallis*, haud *Murus*.

{G}

By the Most Rev'd
DENIS HURLEY,[48]
Archbishop of Durban

I: YOU OR THOU?

On worship the bishops conferred
whether 'you' to 'thou' be preferred:
   till sad to relate,
   Young[49] wrecked the debate
with a Fijian four-letter word.

II

There's many a limerick writ
aglow with conciliar wit;
   but I'm willing to bet
   they'll be denzigered[50] yet
with a whacking anathema sit.

FAREWELL!

{G}

A Rssmo
DIONYSIO HURLEY,
Archiepiscopo Durbaniano

I: UTRUM VOX 'VOS' AN 'TU' USURPATUR?

Inter episcopos de cultu consultatur,
utrum 'vos' an 'tu' præferatur;
at a Iungo Hobartensi
certamen, heu! fidgensi
verbo quadriliterali dissipatur.

II

En facetiæ plures exquisitæ
conciliari sale conditæ;
    quas tamen mox flebitis,
    penes Denzigerum videbitis
anathemate perculsas, nec mite.

VALETE!

THE MODERN CHURCH:
A Conservative's Lament

Latin's gone,
    peace is too;
singin' and shoutin'
    in every pew.

Altar's turned round,
    priest is too,
commentator's yellin'
    "Page twenty-two."

Processions are formin'
    up every aisle;
salvation's organised
    single file.

Rosary's out,
    psalms are in;
hardly ever hear
    a word about sin.

Listen to the Lector,
    hear how he reads:
"Please stop rattlin'
    them Rosary beads!"

Father's puzzled,
    doesn't know his part;
used to know it all
    in Latin by heart.

I hope all the changes
    are just about done,
and they won't drop Bingo
    before I've won.

(American Origin)

DE HUIUS TEMPORIS ECCLESIA
LAUDATORIS TEMPORIS ACTI LAMENTATIO

Exsulat Latinitas,
    paxque iam discessit;
stridor et garrulitas
    e sedibus tumescit.

Versa sunt altaria,
    versus et sacerdos;
audis commentaria:
    numeros dispersos!

Pompæ ad sacraria
    accedunt in fano;
petunt salutaria
    ordine indiano.

Eiecto ian Rosario,
    psalmi increbrescunt;
sermones de vitio
    fere exolescunt.

Lectorem attendite,
    quod legit audire:
"Pro Deum! desistite
    Rosaria tinnire!"

Perturbatur Presbyter
    memoria tam lenta,
quorum olim suaviter
    latine sunt retenta.

Spes est mihi amplius
    nil mutandum fore;
ne tollatur Bingius
    me nondum victore.

(*In latinum versa a Rssmo*
Bernardo Patricio Wall, *Episcopo* Brentvooden)

The Modern Church

A Conservative's

Lament

Latin's gone,
  peace is too;
singin' and shoutin'
  in every pew.

Altar's turned round,
  priest is too,
commentator's yellin'
  'Page twenty-two'.

Processions are formin''
  up every aisle;
salvation's organised
  single file.

Rosary's out,
  psalms are in;
hardly ever hear
  a word about sin.

Listen to the Lector,
  hear how he reads:
'Please stop rattlin'
  them Rosary beads!'

Father's puzzled,
  doesn't know his part;
used to know it all
  in Latin by heart.

I hope all the changes
  are just about done,
and they won't drop Bingo
  before I've won.

(American Origin)

De Huius Temporis Ecclesia

Laudatoris Temporis Acti

Lamentatio

Exsulat Latinitas,
  paxque iam discessit;
stridor et garrulitas
  e sedibus tumescit.

Versa sunt altaria,
  versus et sacerdos;
audis commentaria:
  numeros dispersos!

Pompae ad sacraria
  accedunt in fano;
petunt salutaria
  ordine indiano.

Eiecto iam Rosario,
  psalmi increbrescunt;
sermones de vitio
  fere exolescunt.

Lectorem attendite,
  quod legit audire:
'Pro Deum! desistite
  Rosaria tinnire!'

Perturbatur Presbyter
  memoria tam lenta,
quorum olim suaviter
  latine sunt retenta.

Spes est mihi amplius
  nil mutandum fore;
ne tollatur Bingius
  me nondum victore.

(In latinum versa a
Rssmo Bernardo Patricio
Wall, Episcopo Brentvooden:)

NOTES

1 BERNARD PATRICK WALL (1894–1976), Bishop of Brentwood from 1955 to 1969. His facility in Latin, and sense of humour, enabled him to render in Latin these limericks. McReavy reports that at the end of an audience of the English bishops with John XXIII on 25 November 1962, Wall spontaneously intoned *Ad multos annos*, normally a rousing group chant but on this occasion "rather a flop"; the pope would die little more than six months later.

2 The purplish prose of this title is provided by Bishop Wall only in Latin. It has been translated by the editor.

3 JOHN PATRICK O'LOUGHLIN (1911–1985), priest of the Missionaries of the Sacred Heart of Jesus, Bishop of Darwin from 1949 to 1985. From the records it seems he was not too keen to address the Council, possibly preferring to perfect his limericks, and probably he chose the better part.

4 KARL RAHNER (1904–1984), German Jesuit priest and a most important theologian. On the eve of the Council he was under a cloud in Rome for his progressive theological opinions but John XXIII appointed him a *peritus*, or expert, to the Council at which he was highly influential.
   YVES MARIE-JOSEPH CONGAR (1904–1995), French Dominican priest and theologian. Disciplined for his progressive theological opinions in the 1950s,

John XXIII appointed him to the preparatory commission for the Council. A fervent ecumenist, he had arguably the greatest influence of any one individual at the Council. He was created a cardinal shortly before his death.

HANS KÜNG (1928–), Swiss priest and theologian. The bright young thing of theology in the 1960s, he became ever more aggressively progressive to the point of publicly rejecting papal infallibility. He was stripped of his status as a Catholic theologian in good standing in 1979.

ALFREDO OTTAVIANI (1890–1979), created cardinal in 1953, and head of the Holy Office from 1953 to 1968. Staunchly opposed to the progressive campaign at the Council and considered leader of the traditional element among the Council Fathers, his prelatial motto was *Semper idem*, "Always the same." Effectively blind, he was infamously humiliated on the floor of the Council when, speaking beyond his time, the microphone was switched off on him.

5 PERICLE FELICI (1911–1982), Archbishop of Samosata *i.p.i.*, Secretary-General of the Council, created cardinal in 1967. He was seen as a leader in the curial effort to control the Council's direction. Nevertheless, his sparkling wit, Latin fluency and tireless efficiency won him prolonged applause at the Council's close.

6 LEO JOZEF SUENENS (1904–1996), Archbishop of Malines-Brussels from 1961 to 1979, created cardinal in 1962. He was one of the four moderators of the Council, and a leading progressive. He was one of a group of hostages set to be executed in Louvain by the Nazis near the end of the Second World War but the arrival of Allied forces prevented the execution being carried out. His influence at the Council was so strong that

some fathers dubbed it "The First Council of Malines."
This limerick refers to an intervention by Suenens on
the Council floor on 22 October 1963 calling for women
to be added to a number of laymen already appointed
as auditors to the Council. Douglas Woodruff, then editor of *The Tablet*, is quoted as having remarked that he
had hoped to be appointed a lay auditor at the Council
"but it appears now that my wife will beat me to it."

7 A coadjutor bishop has joint governance of a diocese
beside the diocesan bishop, usually on account of the
latter's poor health. Coadjutors would expect to succeed
their sometimes long-lived diocesan bishops at their
death, but this was not guaranteed.

8 In October 1963, during consideration of the schema
on the Church, there was a sharp division on the question of restoring the diaconate as a permanent order.
The sharpest divisions centred on whether a permanent
deacon could be married. When a vote was taken on
28 September 1964, a large majority voted to restore
the permanent diaconate, and to allow the order to
be conferred on men of mature age who were already
married.

9 In this limerick, as also in IX and XIII, the underlying
issue is episcopal collegiality. While advocated by the
progressive faction, the issue can be seen as essentially
reactionary. As the papacy grew in power through the
middle ages, in no small measure due to monasteries
submitting themselves directly to papal jurisdiction
to avoid interference by local bishops, some bishops
sought to counter-balance papal power by means of
regional synods of bishops and even ecumenical coun-
cils. By the time of the Second Vatican Council the
target of progressive reaction was the Roman Curia

rather than the papacy directly. National and regional conferences of bishops were proposed to counteract the centralized power of the Curia. It was aided by the Council's decision to affirm the sacramentality of the order of bishop, which was no longer seen as a sort of super-priest but a higher and distinct degree of ordination. The argument was that bishops, being successors to the apostles who had comprised a "college" with St Peter, form such a college now with Peter's successor, and enter that college by means of episcopal ordination. One argument employed against collegiality was that it would, in practice, undermine the authority of the bishop in his own diocese by means of the inevitable pressure to conform to the local bishops' conference. The theological question at the heart of the debate is whether the collegiality of bishops is of divine precept, or rather a human construct having moral rather than juridical authority.

10 ANTONIO BACCI (1885–1971), created cardinal in 1960. From 1931 to 1960 he served in the curia as Secretary of Briefs to Princes and of Latin Letters, and excelled even Felici as a Latinist. On 20 and 27 November 1963, during debates on ecumenism, the Moderators rejected his fine distinction between *primatus* and *primatiale* with regard to papal authority, leading to applause from the assembly both times.

11 JOHN CARMEL HEENAN (1905–1975), Archbishop of Liverpool from 1957 to 1963, then Archbishop of Westminster from 1963 to 1975. Created cardinal in 1965, he was not known for radical views. During the Council's third session he helped to found the Saint Paul Conference to oppose elements of the progressive agenda.

12   BERNARD HÄRING (1912–1998), a German priest of the Redemptorist congregation and a moral theologian with progressive views, who served as a *peritus* at the Council. He helped draft the controversial conciliar constitution *Gaudium et spes*. He was attacked without being named by Heenan who spoke against Schema 13 on the Church in the Modern World on which Häring had worked. In it Heenan found clear traces of Häring's support for artificial contraception.

13   In larger or more populous dioceses the diocesan bishop is assisted by one or more auxiliary bishops to whom he delegates authority, usually in a particular area of the diocese. Auxiliaries are given titular dioceses, *in partibus infidelium (i.p.i.)*, defunct dioceses usually in lands no longer Christian, a legal fiction serving the principle that a bishop must be bishop of somewhere. On 11 November 1963, Bishop Antoine Caillot, coadjutor to the bishop of Evreux, argued for the abolition of such titular sees, claiming that "no one but Benedictines know where these titular sees are!"

14   ERNESTO RUFFINI (1888–1967), Archbishop of Palermo from 1945 to 1967, created cardinal in 1946. Considered a conservative, he was an active speaker at the Council often, says McReavy, with "his usual querulous criticisms about defects of clarity and accuracy" in texts. In this limerick reference is made to Ruffini's intervention on 7 October 1963 in which he stated that "it is good and useful to speak of the college of bishops, but we cannot say that this college succeeded the college of the apostles, for the latter did not act collegially except at the Council of Jerusalem."

15   On 11 November 1963, during debate on chapter 2 of the schema on bishops, the concept of setting a

retirement age for bishops was addressed. In a footnote the schema suggested that bishops retire at 75. Archbishop Mingo of Monreale, aged 62, proposed 65 as a mandatory retirement age, calling it *dura lex sed necessaria*, a harsh but necessary law. Two days later Cardinal Suenens pushed for 65 as the mandatory retirement age. Arguments against such a novelty were soon in evidence. Cardinal Ruffini shrewdly reminded the Fathers that John XXIII was already 80 when he was elected pope. Given the demographic of the Council Fathers, it is no surprise that many were uncomfortable on the matter of mandatory retirement. Others suspected, probably correctly, that mandatory retirement would be a means of reshaping the episcopal college. Practical objections were raised such as, who would support a retired bishop in poorer countries and dioceses? Novak noted that "the poverty of the Church in some countries was a revelation to many at the Council." The progressive French commentator Henry Fesquet noted that the proposal was "contrary to the tradition and radical optimism of Christian anthropology." The use of coadjutor bishops was suggested as a compromise. Cardinal Cento proposed a central pension fund for bishops as a practical expression of collegial spirit. On 6 August 1966, in *Ecclesiæ Sanctæ*, Paul VI decreed that bishops would hereafter be "earnestly requested of their own free will to tender their resignation from office not later than at the completion of their 75th year of age." The Bishops of Rome are exempt from this decree.

16 JUAN HERVÁS Y BENET (1905–1982), Prelate Nullius of Ciudad Real in Spain from 1955 to 1976. He made frequent interventions at the council and may be the "young bishop from Spain" referred to in limerick VII. On 12 November 1963 he spoke on abolishing coadjutor bishops.

17   A bishop is traditionally considered to have taken the Church as his spouse, a relationship symbolised by the bishop's ring. For a long time this spousal relationship was understood to be between a bishop and his diocese, which informs the meaning of this limerick, for the coadjutor bishop is not technically the bishop of the diocese in which he is serving. It was part of the argument for collegiality that the bishop's spousal relationship was more correctly seen as being with the universal Church, his appointment to a particular diocese being merely a concrete expression of it. If it were not so, Bishop Luigi Bettazi told the Council Fathers on 12 October 1963, then how could a bishop be transferred from one diocese to another "without feeling he is committing adultery."

18   RICHARD JAMES CUSHING (1895–1970), was Archbishop of Boston from 1944 to 1970, and created cardinal in 1958. A tireless speaker and gifted fund-raiser, he was committed to improving ecumenical and inter-faith relations. The limerick refers to his address on religious liberty on 23 September 1964. Delivered, wrote Xavier Rynne, in "flawless Latin, despite his disclaimers to any knowledge of the language," his speech was applauded.

19   STEPHEN ALOYSIUS LEVEN (1905–1983), from 1955 to 1969 auxiliary bishop in San Antonio, Texas, holding the titular diocese of Bure *i.p.i.*, and from 1969 to 1979 Bishop of San Angelo, Texas. The speech referred to was made on 26 November 1963, during the debate on ecumenism, and described by Michael Novak as *"ad hominem,* chauvinistic, and in some ways graceless;" it incensed many bishops who felt they were his target, as indeed they were.

20 PIETRO PARENTE (1891–1986), Archbishop of Perugia from 1955 to 1959, and then Assessor at the Holy Office from 1959 to 1965, then Secretary of its successor, the Congregation for the Doctrine of the Faith, till 1967 when he was created cardinal. At the Council's theological commission on 11 November 1963, he delivered, in the words of Novak, "an almost hysterical defense of the doctrine that error has no rights."

MICHAEL BROWNE (1887–1971), Master General of the Dominicans from 1955 to 1962, when he was created cardinal and also made Archbishop of Idebessus *i.p.i.* Theologically traditional, a strong opponent of religious liberty and an avid Thomist, when speaking in the Council during the first session in 1962 on Aquinas' insights into the liturgy, Rynne reports that "many of the fathers retreated to Bar Jonah."

21 The conciliar Doctrinal Commission was headed by Cardinal Ottaviani, whose deputy was Cardinal Browne. It produced the schemata on revelation and the Church, but it also claimed the right to vet, and effectively to edit, any draft proposed for a vote by the Council Fathers, an inevitable source of conflict with the other commissions preparing their own drafts. This limerick probably arose from the fractious debate on collegiality in the second session, in particular when Ottaviani objected to the fact that five propositions—four relating to bishops, one to permanent deacons—presented for an indicative vote by the Moderators on 30 October 1963 had not been submitted previously to the Doctrinal Commission, which had competency on dogmatic issues, and which would have "perfected" the text of the propositions.

22 BASIL EDWARD CHRISTOPHER BUTLER (1902–1986), Abbot of Downside from 1946 to 1966, who attended the Council as the Abbot President of

the English Benedictine Congregation (1961–1966). A convert from Anglicanism, and an Oxford graduate, he was fluent in Latin. He was considered progressive.

THOMAS WILLIAM MULDOON (1917–1986), auxiliary bishop of Sydney from 1960 to 1982 under the title of Bishop of Fesseë *i.p.i.* He was one of the younger bishops at the Council and made a number of speeches. He vigorously slapped the Holy Spirit into the editor at the latter's Confirmation, even though the slap was no longer required by the reformed ritual.

The exchange referenced here occurred on 2 December 1963 during the debate on ecumenism. Rynne notes that Muldoon, "in a fit of Irish pugnaciousness" criticised the breast-beating of his brethren regarding the divisions in Christendom, declaring that, "if any feel guilty, let them go to a good confessor but spare the rest of us!" The English, and ex-Anglican, Abbot Butler refused to spare Muldoon, defending the special place of Anglicanism, advocating the "public confession of sins of members of the Church" in matters ecumenical, and speculating that perhaps all the news of the Reformation had not yet reached Australia. Muldoon's reaction is, perhaps tactfully, not recorded.

23   In September 1964 the Vatican admitted 15 female auditors—*auditrices*—to the Council, eight religious and seven laity. However, in November, when a lay male auditor, the American James Norris, suggested that *The Economist* correspondent Barbara Ward address the Council during debate on *Gaudium et spes*, Archbishop Felici told him that while women were welcome to listen, it was "premature" to let them speak.

24   On the eve of the Council the manuals of theology had long taught that there were two sources of divine revelation: Sacred Scripture and Sacred Tradition. After

no little debate, the Council promulgated the constitution *Dei verbum*, in which it taught that there was only one source of divine revelation, the Word of God, composed of scripture and tradition together. O'Loughlin seems to have more sympathy with the pre-conciliar teaching, which may explain his unfavourable view of the new theologians in the next limerick, XXV.

25   On 24 September 1964, a delegation of cardinals presented the skull of St Andrew the apostle to Constantinos, the Greek Orthodox Metropolitan of Patras, as an ecumenical gesture by Paul VI. Tradition holds that St Andrew was martyred in Patras. His skull had been in St Peter's basilica in Rome since 1461, whither it had been brought from Constantinople to preserve it from desecration by the Moslem invaders.

26   MAXIMOS IV SAYEGH [or SAIGH] (1878–1967), Melkite Patriarch of Antioch, was a colourful figure at the Council, making his many speeches not in Latin but French. He resisted the simplistic equation of "Catholic" with the Latin West, and thrice refused a cardinal's hat on the grounds that, notwithstanding the Roman ranking of eastern patriarchs below cardinals, the ancient patriarchs were subordinate only to the pope. In 1965 he finally accepted the red hat when Paul VI arranged matters so that Sayegh was not made part of the clergy of Rome like other cardinals. Maximos declared that, as a result, the college of cardinals had now moved from a Latin institution to the senate of the universal Church. Melchite prelate Elias Zoghbi (cf note 33) was not persuaded.

27   Schema thirteen concerned the Church in the modern world, which took final form as the pastoral constitution *Gaudium et spes*, the last conciliar document

to be promulgated. It was largely the work of French theologians who drew on the thought of Teilhard de Chardin SJ. The progressive German *peritus* Joseph Ratzinger, later Pope Benedict XVI, criticised the decree at the time for, *inter alia*, its secular rather than biblical vocabulary and its implicit equation of Christian hope with a secular conception of human progress.

28 Wall's Latin translation removes O'Loughlin's self-imposed anonymity.

29 BERNARD JAN ALFRINK (1900–1987), Archbishop of Utrecht from 1955-1975, created cardinal in 1960. One of the presidents of the Council and a leading progressive, it was he who ordered the conservative Ottaviani's microphone turned off when the latter ran overtime in responding to Alfrink's own, rather glib, dismissal of Cardinal Godfrey's objections to extending communion from the chalice to the congregation at Mass.

30 LUIGI MARIA CARLI (1914–1986), Bishop of Segni from 1957-1973, then Archbishop of Gaeta from 1973 till his death. An energetic opponent of progressive ideas in the Council, especially the collegiality of bishops, he was said to be "the *porta-voce* [i.e., spokesman] of Cardinal Ottaviani." O'Loughlin's opinion of him is echoed by Rynne, who noted that Carli was one of a number of Italian bishops who seemed to feel that the honour and pre-eminence of the Italian Church "demanded they take an active part in all the discussions." Wiltgen reported that Cardinal Döpfner, one of the four Council moderators, admitted that Carli was the bishop he feared most.

31 JOSEPH-LÉON CARDIJN (1882–1967), Belgian priest and founder of Young Christian Workers, which

in French is *Jeunesse Ouvrière Chrètienne* (JOC), the members of which were known as Jocists. His Catholic social activism was a strong influence at the Council, not least because more than 100 Council fathers had been JOC chaplains. Paul VI created him cardinal in 1965, in time to be able to speak at the last session of the Council, though he had been a member of the preparatory commission for the Council and a *peritus* during it. He made several addresses, the first of which was also the first time he had ever spoken from a written text. His nerves overcome, in his last intervention on 5 October 1965 he was so carried away that he forgot the clock and continued oblivious to the gavel blows of his friend, Cardinal Suenens, who was presiding that day. On this occasion the microphone was not turned off.

32   The limerick refers to Suenens' Council address on 30 September 1965 when he suggested a rite for the annual renewal of marriage vows similar to renewals of baptismal or religious vows.

33   ELIAS ZOGHBI (1912–2008), Melkite Archbishop of Baalbeck, Lebanon. A fervent ecumenist in respect of the Orthodox, he was labelled the Melkites' *enfant terrible*. In his intervention on 30 September 1965, which Fesquet labelled as "one of the most revolutionary of the Council," he advocated following the Orthodox in permitting innocent spouses, adulterously abandoned by their partners, to remarry. On 2 October, Patriarch Maximos IV [cf note 26], perhaps remembering Zoghbi's criticism of his accepting a cardinal's hat earlier in the year, repudiated Zoghbi's position in an interview with *La Croix*.

34   FRANS SIMONS (1908–2002), a priest of the Society of the Divine Word, Bishop of Indore in India

from 1952–1971. A vocal critic of the Roman Curia, his intervention on 7 October 1965 is also described by Fesquet as "one of the most revolutionary of the whole Council." During the debate on the Church's teaching on war he advocated permitting artificial contraception on the basis that a doubtful law does not oblige. He spoke three days after Paul VI had implicitly reaffirmed Catholic teaching on birth control in a speech to the UN General Assembly.

35 *ut patet*, "to be clear"; *placet*, literally, "it pleases," which was the conciliar means of voting in favour of something. Felici, despite his conservative leanings, was very popular for both his skill as Secretary General of the Council, and for his elegant fluency in Latin.

36 ROBERT BLAIR KAISER (1931–2015), having left the Jesuits before ordination to marry, he covered the Council for *Time* magazine. In the wake of the Council he became increasingly active in progressive causes within the Church in America.

MICHAEL NOVAK (1933–2017) covered the second session of the Council for the US *National Catholic Reporter*. His coverage was unabashedly progressive in tone, though in later years he became more conservative in Church matters.

XAVIER RYNNE was the *nom de plume* of Francis Xavier Murphy (1914–2002), an American Redemptorist priest who was teaching in Rome during the Council. His influential coverage of the Council, progressive in its sympathies, was published by the influential journal, *The New Yorker*. Speculation on Rynne's true identity was rife during the Council, and though suspected by some, and questioned on the matter by his superiors, Murphy evaded any admission by means of "casuistry."

37 FERNANDO CENTO (1883–1973), after a long career as a papal nuncio in South America and Europe, was created cardinal in 1958 and appointed Major Penitentiary in 1962, thus heading one of the three tribunals of the Roman Curia. As Major Penitentiary he was responsible for absolving reserved sins and regulating indulgences. He led the debate on the reform of indulgences on 9 November 1965, proposing to abandon the arithmetical calculation of indulgences while retaining some concept of their measure. Among the few to speak in his favour was the Coptic patriarch.

38 When the Council was in session a coffee bar was provided, off the Blessed Sacrament chapel near the sacristy in St Peter's, for use of Council Fathers, *periti* and observers. It was nicknamed Bar-Jonah, a pun on the apostle Peter's cognomen; American English produced a further pun—"Joe's Bar". The bar was a popular refuge from the tedium of much of the Council's business, and the scene of much networking, to use the modern term. There was a second bar, nicknamed Bar-abbas, off the choir chapel on the opposite side of the nave to Bar-Jonah.

39 JOSEPH MARK MCSHEA (1907–1991), Bishop of Allentown from 1961 to 1983. He was relator for the conciliar commission on the religious life, the schema for which was vigorously opposed in the third session by those who found it too conservative. Rynne notes that McShea's argument in defence of the schema "was hardly in conformity with the facts—[but] played an important part in saving the text."

This dedication was composed in Latin without an English translation, and so has been translated by the editor.

40 The original has "Alantown", though in fact it is Allentown. The error is presumably due the use of "Alan" in its Latin name.

41 WILLIAM GORDON WHEELER (1910–1998), Coadjutor Bishop of Middlesbrough from 1964 to 1966, and then Bishop of Leeds from 1966 to 1985. A convert Anglican clergyman, he read history at Oxford. As a Catholic bishop he was liturgically traditional and, while he accepted the liturgical reforms in the wake of the Council, his preference in private was for the old Mass. Theudalis was his titular see while coadjutor in Middlesbrough.

42 *Objections to Roman Catholicism*, edited by Michael de la Bedoyère (London, 1964), was a collection of essays by progressive Catholics, including Magdalen Goffin and John Todd. Goffin rejected the existence of hell and the eternal loss of the vision of God, which she saw as promoting faith in a God which "no one in his senses would wish to see." In his 1965 review of the book, Kenelm Foster OP opined that generally a book with such a title by Catholic contributors would follow the formula, "yes, but...."; this book instead adopted the formula "yes, *and*...."!

43 ARTHUR MICHAEL RAMSEY (1904–1988), the 100th Archbishop of Canterbury from 1961 to 1974. He was active in Anglican ecumenism.
    JOHN ARTHUR THOMAS ROBINSON (1919–1983), Anglican Bishop of Woolwich from 1959 to 1969. His book *Honest to God*, published in 1963, rejected the notion of a transcendent God in favour of God as the "ground of being". Archbishop Ramsey hurriedly published a response critical, but not entirely dismissive, of Robinson's book.

44   PAUL GAUTHIER [*sic*] (1914–2002), priest of the diocese of Dijon and theologian, who would later leave the priesthood to marry. In 1963 he published, first in French and in English translation the following year, *Christ, the Church and the Poor*. Two thousand copies were distributed to the Council Fathers. The book partly inspired more than 40 Council Fathers to issue *The Pact of the Catacombs: A Poor Servant Church* in November 1965, and laid the foundations for the liberation theology that emerged a few years later.

45   GEORGE PATRICK DWYER (1908–1987), Bishop of Leeds from 1957 to 1965, then Archbishop of Birmingham from 1965 to 1981. He is accounted the prime mover in the implementation of the use English in the liturgy in England and Wales as part of the post-conciliar reforms. He did not always embrace the reform agenda with serenity. Fittingly, he was buried on the feast of Our Lady of Ransom according to the new calendar, which feast was saved from the reformers' knife by his intervention.

46   CYRIL CONRAD COWDEROY (1905–1976), Bishop of Southwark from 1949, and from 1965 its Archbishop until his sudden death. He converted to Catholicism as a boy in company with his mother. As a bishop he was known to be a calm and tender pastor. Liturgically traditional, he was grieved by many of the changes in the wake of the Council; as a seminarian he lamented the replacement of the old Roman-cut vestments with those of the gothic revival.

47   With the advent of the vernacular it was inevitable that there would be debate as to what register of English to use. In 1967 Burns & Oates published an altar missal in binder form, with removable inserts

available in both "you" and "thou" versions. In France, a comparable reaction arose over the use of *tu* instead of *vous* when addressing God.

48   DENIS EUGENE HURLEY (1915–2004), an Oblate of Mary Immaculate, and Archbishop of Durban from 1951 to 1992. When first ordained a bishop in 1946 he was only 31 and was at that time the youngest bishop in the world. He helped found ICEL (the International Commission on English in the Liturgy) in 1963, and in 1975 was elected its chairman. In 1961 he was appointed to the central commission preparing for the Council on the mistaken belief that he was still president of the South African bishops' conference. He was a leading advocate of active participation by the laity in the liturgy. That he was never made a cardinal is attributed to his muted criticism of Paul VI's *Humanæ Vitæ* in 1968.

49   (Sir) GUILFORD CLYDE YOUNG (1916–1988), Archbishop of Hobart from 1955 till his death in 1988. Ordained priest at 22, and bishop at 31, at which time he took the mantle as the youngest bishop in the world. He excelled as a student at Propaganda Fide's Roman university. He was prominent in liturgical reform, and in 1963, with Archbishop Hurley, helped to found ICEL. As early as 1960 he had required dialogue Masses in his diocese and had implemented ritual reforms that anticipated some post-conciliar reforms. Hurley's limerick seems to refer to a commission meeting rather than an exchange on the Council floor. The Fijian four-letter word has so far evaded certain identification by the editor, but *boci* or *boce* are likely candidates.

50   "Denzinger" is the customary shorthand for the *Enchiridion Symbolorum Definitionum et Declarationum de Rebus Fidei et Morum*, "The Handbook of Creeds,

Definitions, and Declarations on Matters of Faith and Morals," first edited by Heinrich Denzinger in 1854, and appearing in 36 further, and expanded, editions up to 1991. It has the reputation of being the definitive compendium of Catholic dogma.

BIBLIOGRAPHY

Fesquet, Henri, *The Drama of Vatican II: The Ecumenical Council June 1962–December 1965*, New York, 1967.

Johnson, Cuthbert Peter, *Vatican II As I Saw It: Letters, Journal, Diary and Papers of Lawrence Leslie McReavy*, Farnborough, 2015.

Novak, Michael, *The Open Church: Vatican II, Act II*, New York, 1964.

Rynne, Xavier, *Letters from Vatican City: Vatican Council II (First Session): Background and Debates*, New York, 1963. –

—, *The Second Session: The Debates and Decrees of Vatican Council II, September 29 to December 4, 1963*, London, 1964.

—, *The Third Session: The Debates and Decrees of Vatican Council II, September 14 to November 21, 1964*, London, 1965.

—, *The Fourth Session: The Debates and Decrees of Vatican Council II, September 14 to December 8, 1965*, London, 1966.

Wiltgen, Ralph, *The Rhine Flows into the Tiber: A History of Vatican II*, New York, 1967.

About the Editor

DOM HUGH SOMERVILLE KNAPMAN IS a Benedictine monk and priest of Douai Abbey near Reading, England. He is the author of *Ecumenism of Blood: Heavenly Hope for Earthly Communion* (Paulist Press, 2018). Currently he is pursuing doctoral studies at St Mary's University, Twickenham.

Lightning Source UK Ltd.
Milton Keynes UK
UKHW041154231120
373920UK00015B/847/J